To my long little dogie

Illustrations copyright © 2005 Richard A. Goldberg

Designed by Karine Syvertsen

Copyright © 2005
Peter Pauper Press, Inc.
202 Mamaroneck Avenue
White Plains, NY 10601
All rights reserved
ISBN 1-59359-963-3
Printed in China
7 6 5 4 3 2 1

Visit us at www.peterpauper.com

To:

From:

ZEN COWBOY

or
How to Become One
with the Herd

Michael W. Domis
Illustrated by Richard A. Goldl

 Peter Pauper Press, Inc.
WHITE PLAINS, NEW YORK

Contents

INTRODUCTION 5

COW-ANS 10

TALES FROM THE WAY OF THE DUSTY TRAIL .16

A Parable: Be the Cow 18

A Parable: Be One With the Herd 22

A Parable: Go With the Flow 28

A Parable: Mu-vin' Along 34

A Parable: Identification 39

THE SINGING TAOBOY 45

ZENFIGHT AT THE I'M OK, YOU'RE OK CORRAL .51

ZEN FIGHTERS AND OUTLAWS 60

Zen Fighters 63

Zen Outlaws 67

COW-KU 71

GLOSSARY 77

Introduction

What is a Zen cowboy? Well, pardner, pull up a rock, set a spell, start the tea ceremony, and let me tell you all about it.

You know what a cowboy is, right? A cowboy is a lot of things. He tends the cows, ensuring their safety. He herds them when the need arises. He leads his cattle to the green pastures. It is his udder vocation.

But a Zen cowboy, well, my friend, a Zen cowboy is someone who's got it all figured out. He's the one who's not only home on the range, but home in the city and the suburbs as well. The Zen cowboy, or Taoboy, has mastered and given up all his desires in his quest for ultimate enlightenment. He contemplates the Mu, or Nothingness, in order to free himself of his illusions. The Zen cowboy has become one with the herd, and the range, and heck, just about everything.

So, you wanna try and become a Zen cowboy? That's a right noble aspiration, young'un. Tell you what, you just pay

attention to what follows in this here book, and you'll be headed on the right track.

Saddle up, pardner, we've got some enlightenment ahead of us. We're gonna head on down to the "I'm OK; You're OK" corral for a few cow chips of enlightenment.

8

Sing along, now:

"Ommm, ommm on the range,
Where the cows will
be chanting all day.
Where everything's one,
'Cause that steak is well-done,
And the mind is not
cloudy all day."

Cow-ans

What follows are what I call "cow-ans." They're based on the Zen things called koans. Koans are little riddles and whatnot meant to get you to thinkin' about the Mu. You remember the Mu, right—the idea of nothingness? Well, by asking students one of these questions, you force them to contemplate a mystery that has no answer. By doing that, they get a whole heck of a lot closer to letting

go of desire and ego. Anyway, read
and think, Taoboy.

*What is the sound of
one Mu cow mooing?*

What is the nature of grass?

Is the hokey-pokey what it's all about?

Why do they call it
square dancing when we
go around in circles?

WWBD— What would Buddha do?

Can you ever step in the same
cow-pie twice?

**If you give a cow a fish,
you're wasting your time.
But, if you teach a cow to fish,
you can at least make some
money charging people to
see a fishing cow.**

How can two people be at
one with everything?

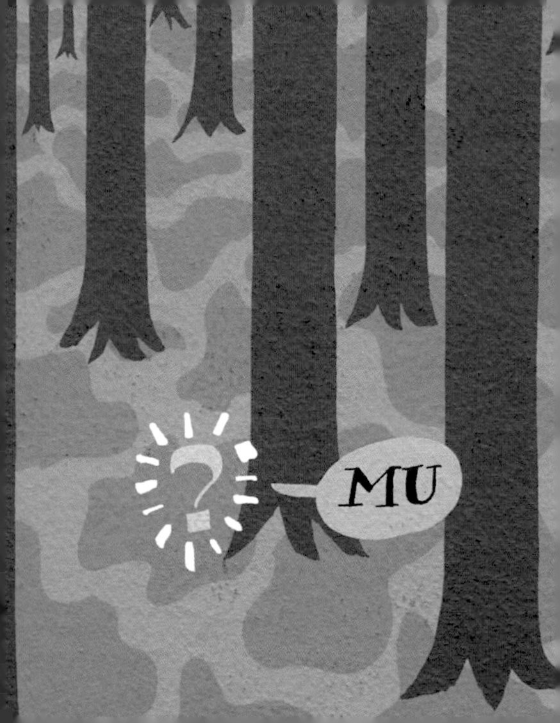
MU

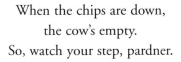

When the chips are down,
the cow's empty.
So, watch your step, pardner.

**If a cow moos in the forest,
and nobody is there to hear it,
does the cow really exist?**

Tales from the Way of the Dusty Trail

Well, let me introduce myself afore I get to jawin' too much. The students around these here parts call me sensei, or master, but you can call me Tex. I've been riding herd on cattle and Zen acolytes for a powerful long time, it seems like—'bout 30 years, I reckon. I seen a lot of kids come through here, and herded a lot of cows. I guess I've become enlightened along the way, and occasionally I feel like I'm one with everything, but mostly I just do what I do best.

But, enough about me, let's get started with a few stories I tell to the new students about becomin' a Taoboy.

A PARABLE:
Be the Cow

I was out working the herd one day, a fine summer day as I recall, when this young greenhorn sauntered on up to me and asked, "Sensei, how do I become a Zen cowboy?"

Well, I looked him over. Seems he was outfitted right to be a regular cowboy, but I had to find out if he was ready for the first step in letting go and becoming.

"Do you know how to rope and ride?" I asked.

"I do," the greenhorn replied.

"Do you know what it is to be a cow?" I asked.

Well, he looked a might flummoxed at that question. "How can I be a cow?" he asked.

"Get down on all fours," I said. (I'm not above a little visual aid, every now and again.)

He did what I told him, which was good.

"Act like a cow," I instructed.

Well, he looked up at me, kinda shrugged, and then he commenced to mooing. He mooed, and ate some grass, and pawed at the ground.

I couldn't help it. When he did that, I about fell over laughing.

The kid got up, all red in the face and whatnot. "This is foolish," he said. "I am not a cow."

"Very good," says I. "You have taken the first step toward cow-lightenment."

Now, that is the first step: figuring out what you are not. However, the next step is much harder: figuring out what you are, and what you want to be.

A PARABLE:
Be One With the Herd

Of course, there are lessons to be learned everywhere when you're doing the job of a cowboy. Even something as simple as herding cattle can reveal some mysteries. Why, I remember one night, when we had settled down by the campfire after a long day of driving cattle, one young student stirred the ashes of the fire and asked, "Sensei, what is the secret to herding cattle?"

"You must become one with the herd," I said. "After you do that, herdin' cattle is easy."

"How do you become one with the herd?" the young student queried.

I smiled. "Think like a cow."

"Cows don't think," said one of my older students. "They just are."

"That's very true," I replied. "But, I wasn't a'talkin' to you, ya durn fool. You may now become one with a shovel and muck out the corral. And recite your Sutras while you're at it."

Well, he grumbled a mite, but my students know better than to disobey, so he took the shovel and went to it. I sent the younger kid with him to watch.

After a bit, the kid returned.

"How's he doin'?" I asked.

"Well, he's still at it, but he fell

down about a dozen times right in the cow-flop. He don't look too good. He smells to high heaven, and he's really angry."

"And what have you learned, kid?"

"Well, I've learned that sometimes it's best to keep your mouth shut, unless you like shoveling manure."

"Good. And?"

"I've also learned that you should never kick a warm cow patty."

I chuckled. "That's pure wisdom, son. Anything else?"

"Well, I also figger that while it's important to become one with the herd, it's not necessary to become one with the herd's manure."

"Good job, kid," said I. "You might just become a Taoboy after all."

Moral: To tap into universal mind, rise above the crap.

A PARABLE:
Go With the Flow

Mind you, the Taoboy life ain't all solving mysteries. Sometimes, it can be right dangerous. However, there's lessons to be learned there, too. Why, one night I remember spilling my green tea from that awful shaking of thundering hooves.

"Who allowed these consarned cattle to stampede?" I yelled. I got no answer, of course.

"All right," I said. "Y'all gather around me and hunker down."

They did, and jumped back up just as quick. I shook my head. "Do I have to teach you everything?" I asked. "Don't you fools know not to squat with your spurs on?"

They looked embarrassed, and rightfully so.

"Never mind about that. Will somebody please tell me why the cows are being allowed to stampede like this?"

"Sensei," said a young'un, "we do

not know why the cows stampede. These things just happen."

"Fool!" I yelled. "Everything has a reason. Now, git your horse, ride on ahead, and rope the lead cow."

We all whooped, jumped into our saddles, and rounded up them dogies. After we got the herd settled, I gathered the students together again. "Now, what's the best way to stop a stampede?" I asked.

The student I called a fool puffed up with pride and said, "You rope the lead cow."

"You're still a fool!" I yelled at him. I reckon' I was a bit put out from spilling my tea and all. "The best way to stop a stampede," I began.

"Is to not let it happen in the first place?" another student asked.

"Excellent. That is exactly the answer," I told him. "You may have first choice at dinner this evening."

He looked mighty proud of himself, and rightfully so. See, it takes a real Zen cowboy to thwart a herd's desire to stampede. Cows are not the brightest critters, and they're easily spooked. I reckon the same could be said for people, as well.

A PARABLE:
Mu-vin' Along

I reckon you're feelin' pretty enlightened now, aintcha? You figure this Taoboy stuff is pretty easy, right? Think again.

"Sensei," one of my students asked me recently, "when will I know I have reached nirvana?"

"When you can solve the riddle of herdin' cats," I told him.

"No one can herd cats," the student replied.

"Ahhh," I said, "not so. Herdin' cats is difficult, but not impossible. It requires the entire skills of a Zen cowboy to solve the riddle of herdin' cats."

"I will take on this task," said the student and, so saying, he left.

I didn't see him for about three years.

When he finally returned, he said, "Master, one cannot herd cats."

"Did you try appealin' to their higher nature?" I inquired.

"Cats don't seem to have a higher nature," the student replied.

"Very good. But, did you try appealin' to their baser nature?" I asked.

"Cats don't have that, neither," the student said.

"Well, what do they have, then?"

"They have nothing. Cats just are," the kid said.

"Cats just are what?" I asked.

"Cats are just damned hard to herd," he said.

"You're learning," I said. "Welcome back."

Moral: We discriminate between what is ours to do, and what is not. Bending others to our will is not the Taoboy way.

A PARABLE:
Identification

Well, you're almost there, pardner. I just have one final little story for y'all. Listen up, now.

"I have a riddle, students. There are three cowboys in a truck. How can you tell which one is the real Zen cowboy?"

My students considered this.

"Is it the one driving, because he steers the correct course between ego and desire?"

"No, but a good answer," I told him.

"I know," said another student. "It is the one on the outside, because he becomes one with the unfolding landscape."

"No, but excellent thinking," I said.

"Well then," said the third and youngest student, "it must be the one in the middle, but I cannot think why."

"You are right about where he's a'sittin'. But, you must do what he does to figger it out. I tell you what. You three deliver this here load of grain to the north field. You," I said, pointin' to the one who got the right answer, "sit in the correct place to be a Zen cowboy and cogitate on it. Get on, now."

After they delivered the grain and got back, I questioned him again. "Did you sit in the middle?"

"I did," said the youngest student.

41

"What did you do while sitting there?"

"I thought about the riddle of being and nothingness, and found a portion of my ego that I must get rid of."

"Excellent. But, how could you have time to do this when I told you to deliver that grain?"

"Well," the student replied, "Since I was sittin' in the middle I didn't have to drive, and I didn't have to get out and open all them gates.

So, I could just meditate and free my mind."

"Good on you, kid," I said. "This is the way of the Zen cowboy."

"But, Sensei, is the same thing true for all vehicles?"

"Well," said I, "it is. But there is one thing to consider."

"What's that?" he asked.

"Whoever's doin' the drivin' has to make sure the Carma doesn't run over the Dogma."

The Singing Taoboy

Did I tell you I write music? Well, now, that ain't entirely correct. I re-write music to be perzact. See, being a cowboy, I listen to Country and Western music. I take some of my favorite songs and re-write them as Zen cowboy songs.

For example, one of my favorites is by a group called the Highwaymen. They put out a little ditty called *Ghost Riders in the Sky*. I rewrote that as *Zen Riders in the Ether*. Aww, I know it ain't gonna get me on the Grand Ol' Opry, but it is slap dang amusin'.

Here are some others I've rewritten.
You'll find the original song title in
parentheses.

Your Cheatin' Aura

(Your Cheatin' Heart)

A Boy Named Mu

(A Boy Named Sue)

I'm So Enlightened
I Could Fly

(I'm So Lonesome I Could Cry)

At One With the Twist and Shout

(Down at the Twist and Shout)

Will the Karma Be Derailed?

(Will the Circle Be Unbroken?)

I Never Promised You a Zen Garden

(I Never Promised You a Rose Garden)

I Will Always Enlighten You

(I Will Always Love You)

Third Eye Crying in the Rain

(Blue Eyes Crying in the Rain)

Cool Tao

(Cool Water)

What Is the Nature of the Green, Green Grass of Home?

(The Green, Green Grass of Home)

And my favorite of all time is:

Mu Skinner Blues

(Mule Skinner Blues).

Zenfight at the I'm OK, You're OK Corral

Well, now, I have to tell you, not every student I've ever had has used his powers for good. Some of those boys get a little enlightenment and then get to thinkin' that they're all that, if you know what I mean. Eventually, it leads to trouble.

There was this one time when we was all gathered down at Miss Kitty's Chai Palace and Shiatsu Massage

Parlor. We Taoboys had just driven a herd in from Tokyo, and the boys needed to relax and refuel. We were just settlin' down to our second cup of green tea when I heard the deputy come stompin' in through the door.

"Marshal!" he yells. "There's a'fixin' to be a Zenfight down to the corral."

"Now, now, deputy," says the marshal, "just calm down and tell me what's happening."

"Bad Bodhi Bob called Slim Nagano an unenlightened son of a dog. They're headed to the corral right now to settle it."

The marshal left with the deputy, and me and the boys followed. The young'uns had never seen a Zenfight before, and I figgered they ought to.

When we got there, Bad Bob and Slim were standing about 10 paces apart. I could see that Slim was nervous but he was trying to find his center. Bad Bob just chuckled and waited.

Slim got centered, opened his eyes, and said, "Make your move."

Bad Bob nodded, jumped up, tucked his legs under himself and extended his

arms. He hit the ground with a "thud."
When the dust cleared, we all saw that
he was sitting calmly, legs crossed, with
his arms resting on his knees in full
meditation.

The crowd oohed and aaahed.

"Not bad," I said. I looked at Slim,
and gave him a wink of encouragement.

Slim nodded, jumped up and came
down with a loud-
er "thud," but
in full lotus
position, wrists
on knees, palms upward,
and the middle finger of

each hand lightly touching its thumb. A steady "ommm-mmm" came from Slim.

The crowd erupted into applause.

Bad Bob opened one eye, took a look at Slim, reached into his vest, and pulled out a-a-a crystal.

"Ain't those illegal?" asked one of my students.

"Now you know why they call him 'Bad Bob'," I replied.

Well, Bob commenced to twirling that crystal which caught the noon-day sun and heli-arced all over the place.

Several bystanders were temporarily blinded. One of the ladies fainted.

Slim's eyes flew open as the colors hit them. We figgered he had lost all concentration and was a goner for sure. But, he sat there, eyes open, and commenced to chanting again. And the weirdest thing happened. All the colors started to head right toward him. It was like he was drawing them in, right through his eyes. Soon, there was a steady stream of every color of the rainbow flowing from the crystal right into Slim.

"Stop it!" Bad Bob shouted. "You're ruinin' my crystal. I paid a hundred bucks for this thing on the Prairie Shopping Network."

But, before you knew it, all the color was gone from the crystal and into Slim. With a tiny "pop" the crystal turned to dust.

"That'll do'er," I told my students. "Bob's done for."

Slim opened his mouth and all those colors he had inside streamed out

toward Bad Bob. They wrapped themselves around Bob, and just sank in. Bob fell backwards from the impact. Slim smiled, and continued to chant.

"Is he gonna be OK?" one of my students inquired.

"I reckon," I said. "For awhile, he'll be the happiest, friendliest, nicest guy in town. Unfortunately, once it wears off, he'll just be Bad Bodhi Bob again. Enlightenment never lasts with those types."

"What types?" a student asked.

"The types what think that things, rather than the human spirit, help us attain enlightenment."

Zen Fighters and Outlaws

I've known a heap of people in my life, I can tell you. And, like I said, I've taught a passel of students what it is to be a Zen Taoboy. Along the way, I've run across a few people that it's been my distinct pleasure to have known.

PAUL "SLIM" WHITBEY

FLINT "PALE RIDER" URADEDMAN

61

These folks belong in a class I call "Zen Fighters." They have successfully fought, and continue to fight, all the desires and ego that keep them from being one with everything. Here's my short list of them right noble folks.

Zen Fighters

KONAMU "TEX" MYATA
13th level Zen Fighter

CLAIM TO FAME: While explaining the essence of Cow to a student, Tex suddenly manifested as a ball of pure energy.

OFTEN HEARD SAYING: "To be nothing is really something."

PAUL "SLIM" WHITBEY

10th level Zen Fighter

CLAIM TO FAME: Only American to reach level ten of Zen Cowboy Mastery.

OFTEN HEARD SAYING: "Hey, hot dog man, make me one with every-thing."

KINSASHA "BELLE" NAGAMA
14th level Zen Fighter

CLAIM TO FAME: Only female to ever attain such a ranking, she was famous for writing *Songs of Being and Nothingness* which included the hit: *Mu, Mu, Mu Yourself, Gently Down the Stream of Consciousness.*

OFTEN HEARD SAYING: "I don't mean it then, if it ain't got that Zen. Do wop do wop do wop."

THE LONE ENLIGHTENER

Mystery level Zen Fighter

CLAIM TO FAME: Rides silently into a didactically difficult situation, drops a few well-chosen *bon mots*, and then rides away, leaving his students to wonder: "Who was that masked man?" "I don't know, but he left some silver enlightenment."

OFTEN HEARD SAYING: "Heigh-ho Buddha boy, Aaaaawaaaayyyyy!!!!"

Zen Outlaws

Now, you can't have the good without the bad; that's a Karmic kind of thing. That means: for every noble Zen fighter out there, there's at least one Zen outlaw. A Zen outlaw is lower than a snake's belly in a wheel rut, karmically speakin', of course. They've learned enough about Zen to become dangerous. But more than that, they THINK they know a lot more than they do. Kinda like politicians, ya know?

If you see any of these sidewinders, you steer right clear, y'hear?

RAYNO "THE GIPPER" RAYGO
40th President of the Zen Cowboy Council and Cheerleading Society

CLAIM TO FAME: Former host of *Zen Valley Days.*

OFTEN HEARD SAYING: "Cows cause more pollution than trees, ya know."

JANN "THE DUKE" WAY-BO

CLAIM TO FAME: "The Duke" claims to be so advanced, and have knowledge of Zen and self so great, that no one really understands him. In actuality, however, he's a weatherman out of Secaucus.

OFTEN HEARD SAYING: "Yes, but the Mu of the Purple Kumquat forbids it."

FLINT "PALE RIDER" URADEDMAN

CLAIM TO FAME: An ardent student of the Sutras, he has written several books filled with complex, introspective Zen cowboy riddles (cow-ans) designed not to enlighten, but to confuse students.

OFTEN HEARD SAYING: "I have just one question for you: Do you feel enlightened? Well, do you, punk?"

Cow-ku

Based on the ancient poetical form of haiku, these verses have been handed down through the ages by various Zen Taoboys.

The campfire burns bright.
The cattle are contented.
I am one with all.

Wind is sweeping down
the plain. My ego yearns to
accompany it.

This horse does not wish
to go where I want to go.
So, I go with him.

Floating, on a sea
of grass. Freed from constraints of
self. I am nothing.

To herd is to be.
To be is to herd, as well.
A circle of Zen.

What's the Tao of cow?
To graze and chew cud with joy,
Contented and free.

The sun shines on the
steaming cow-pie,
showing us
the essence of cow.

Rope that dogie, kid.
Tie him and brand him, as well.
Take joy in your work.

I'm a Zen cowhand,
From the Rio Grande, so my
Ego's small, yet grand.

Mindful of the cows,
I am mindful of the Mu.
Moo, Mu cows, moo, moo.

Glossary

This here's the place where you can look to find some words you might not know the meaning of.

BODHI: Enlightenment.

CONSARNED: A polite expletive. Suitable for use in front of the women-folk and children.

COW CHIP: The end product of all that hay the cows have been chewing.

COW-FLOP: See Cow chip.

DOGIE: Little calf in a herd of cattle.

DOGMA: A principle or belief thought to be absolutely true, without exception.

FLUMMOXED: Perplexed confusion.

GREENHORN: An inexperienced Taoboy. A newbie.

HUNKER: To squat close to the ground.

JAWIN': Talking or conversing.

KARMA: The total effect of one's actions and conduct during successive incarnations.

MU: Nothingness.

NIRVANA: The big kahuna of enlightenment.

PERZACT: Perfectly exact.

SENSEI: Master. That's me.

SIDEWINDER: A small, poisonous snake that doesn't slither, but moves diagonally forward in a series of S-shaped motions. Also, a scurrilous individual.

SUTRA: The hit parade of Buddhist stories.

TAO: The basic, eternal principle of the

universe that transcends physical reality. The source of all being, non-being, and change.

ZEN: From the Chinese Chán, meaning quietude. It's the idea that you can attain enlightenment through meditation, the inward voyage of self-discovery, and big skies.